Festivals *of the* World

HAITI

Gareth Stevens Publishing
MILWAUKEE

Written by
ROSELINE NGCHEONG-LUM

Edited by
AUDREY LIM

Designed by
HASNAH MOHD ESA

Picture research by
SUSAN JANE MANUEL

First published in North America in 1999 by
Gareth Stevens Publishing
1555 North RiverCenter Drive, Suite 201
Milwaukee, Wisconsin 53212 USA

For a free color catalog describing Gareth
Stevens' list of high-quality books and multimedia
programs, call
1-800-542-2595 (USA)
or 1-800-461-9120 (Canada).
Gareth Stevens Publishing's Fax: (414) 225-0377.

© TIMES EDITIONS PTE LTD 1999
Originated and designed by
Times Books International
an imprint of Times Editions Pte Ltd
Times Centre, 1 New Industrial Road
Singapore 536196
Printed in Malaysia

Library of Congress Cataloging-in-Publication Data:
NgCheong-Lum, Roseline, 1962–.
Haiti / by Roseline NgCheong-Lum.
p. cm. — (Festivals of the world)
Includes bibliographical references and index.
Summary: Describes how the culture of Haiti is
reflected in its many festivals, including Carnival,
Feast of St. James, and Independence Day.
ISBN 0-8368-2015-0 (lib. bdg.)
1. Festivals—Haiti—Juvenile literature. 2. Haiti—
Social life and customs—Juvenile literature.
[1. Festivals—Haiti. 2. Holidays—Haiti. 3. Haiti—
Social life and customs.] I. Title. II. Series.
GT4826.A2N43   1998
394.2697294—dc21   98-13803

1 2 3 4 5 6 7 8 9 03 02 01 00 99

CONTENTS

It's Festival Time . . .

No festival in Haiti is complete without music, dancing, and feasting. Haitians have many occasions to feast since they celebrate both Christian and **voodoo** festivals. Want to show off your pet "monster" or take part in a lantern procession? Or would you prefer to listen to the rousing music of the Rara bands or participate in a pilgrimage to Saut d'Eau? Come to Haiti and enjoy the feasts!

WHERE'S HAITI?

Haiti is located on the western side of the island of Hispaniola in the West Indies. Its closest neighbor is the Dominican Republic, which occupies the rest of the island. Haiti is a very mountainous country, and its

coastline is ragged with steep cliffs. This former French colony was the second country in the world, after the United States, to declare its independence.

Who are the Haitians?

Today's Haitians are descendants of African slaves who were brought to the island in the seventeenth and eighteenth centuries to work on sugarcane plantations. Less than 5 percent of the population are mulattoes, or people of mixed African-European descent. Many Haitians have fled the poverty and strife of their homeland to seek a better future in Europe or North America.

Haitians are cheerful people even though they live in one of the poorest countries in the world.

4

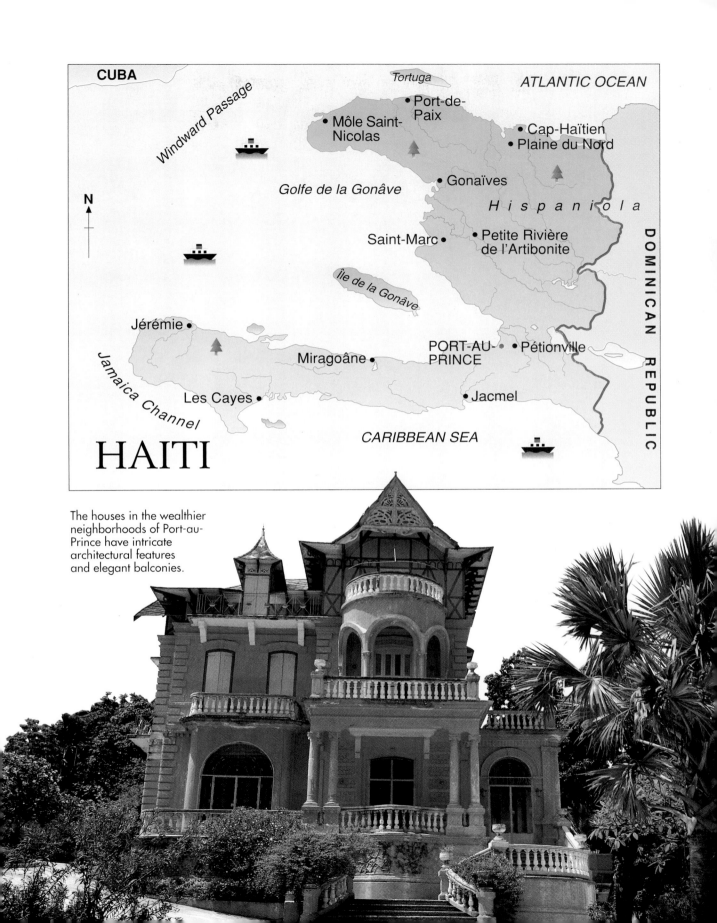

CUBA

Tortuga

ATLANTIC OCEAN

Windward Passage

• Port-de-Paix

• Môle Saint-Nicolas

• Cap-Haïtien
• Plaine du Nord

• Gonaïves

Golfe de la Gonâve

H i s p a n i o l a

Saint-Marc •

• Petite Rivière de l'Artibonite

Île de la Gonâve

N

Jérémie •

Miragoâne •

PORT-AU-PRINCE

• Pétionville

Jamaica Channel

Les Cayes •

• Jacmel

CARIBBEAN SEA

DOMINICAN REPUBLIC

HAITI

The houses in the wealthier neighborhoods of Port-au-Prince have intricate architectural features and elegant balconies.

WHEN'S THE FEAST?

Smile! We're going to have our picture taken!

SPRING

- ✪ **CARNIVAL AND RARA**
- ✪ **EASTER**
- ✪ **DEATH OF TOUSSAINT L'OUVERTURE**—This public holiday, on April 7th, commemorates the death of the first Haitian to win independence for the country.
- ✪ **SPRING FESTIVAL**—Haiti celebrates this festival from May 1st to 4th with much feasting and dancing. Every town holds a parade, and officials join in the march. Part of the Spring Festival is Labor Day, also called Agricultural Day in Haiti.
- ✪ **HARVEST FESTIVAL**

SUMMER

- ✪ **SAUT D'EAU**
- ✪ **FEAST OF SAINT JAMES**
- ✪ **FEAST OF SAINT ANNE**
- ✪ **ASSUMPTION OF THE VIRGIN MARY**—This Catholic feast day on August 15th is also an important public holiday in Haiti. Catholics attend masses devoted to Mary, the mother of Jesus Christ.

AUTUMN

- ⚙ **FEAST OF SAINT ANDREW**
- ⚙ **DEATH OF JEAN-JACQUES DESSALINES**—On October 17th, Haiti commemorates the death of the man who proclaimed its independence.
- ⚙ **DAY OF THE DEAD**
- ⚙ **VERTIÈRES DAY**—Military parades and speeches highlight this Armed Forces Day.

WINTER

- ⚙ **MANGER YAM**—This celebration takes place on November 25th and is the most important harvest festival in Haiti. *Manger yam* [mahn-djay YAM] means "eating yam." This root vegetable plays an important role in the Haitian diet, so peasants enjoy feasting, singing, and dancing on this day. Before the festivities begin, a voodoo priest performs a ceremony of prayers to the dead and to voodoo spirits.
- ⚙ **THE FOUNDING OF HAITI**—December 5th marks the day, in 1492, when Christopher Columbus landed on Hispaniola.
- ⚙ **CHRISTMAS**
- ⚙ **NEW YEAR'S DAY**
- ⚙ **INDEPENDENCE AND HEROES DAY**

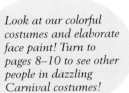

Look at our colorful costumes and elaborate face paint! Turn to pages 8–10 to see other people in dazzling Carnival costumes!

7

CARNIVAL AND RARA

One of the grandest festivals in Haiti is Carnival. This huge party lasts six weeks. It starts on January 6th and ends on Shrove Tuesday in February.

Come on and celebrate

Every weekend during Carnival, the Haitian government holds free open-air concerts in various parts of Port-au-Prince, the capital of the country. Celebrations reach their peak, with much feasting and dancing, during the last four days of Carnival. Since Carnival is one of the biggest events of the year, preparations begin very early. Some adults and children start making their costumes and masks in October the previous year!

Carnival dancers wear colorful costumes and hats! Turn to pages 28 and 29 to find out how to make a hat as colorful as this dancer's.

These people are waiting for Carnival to begin.

Musicians add to the festive atmosphere at Carnival time.

Mardi Gras parades

Although parades are organized every Sunday during Carnival, the most elaborate ones, called Mardi Gras [MAHR-dee GRAH], take place on Shrove Tuesday. *Mardi Gras* means "fat Tuesday," and Shrove Tuesday is the last day before Lent, a 40-day period of fasting and penance observed by many Christian religions. Mardi Gras is the most exciting time of Carnival. Revelers dressed in colorful costumes and masks follow walking bands, called ***bandes-à-pieds*** [bahn-dah-PEEAY], through the streets, dancing and singing with abandon. An elected Carnival king and queen parade through the streets in beautifully decorated floats.

See my monster

Children participate in Carnival by showing off little wooden boxes decorated with paint and tissue paper. Each box, called a **lamayote** [lah-mah-YOT], contains a small pet—or a "monster." The monster usually turns out to be a freshly caught lizard, bug, or mouse, or some other small animal. The children run around the streets in costumes and masks, blowing whistles and stopping passersby to show them their lamayotes. In return, the children get a few coins.

Even a Carnival parade held at night is colorful and exciting.

Children having fun during Carnival, dressing up, dancing around, and showing off their lamayotes.

The Rara

Rara, also known as the "peasant festival," immediately follows Carnival. Every weekend during Lent, voodoo followers celebrate Rara. Lent refers to the 40 days before Easter.

Rara bands are made up of a band leader, a musical group, a queen and her attendants, a choir, and food sellers. The bands dress in red and carry a red flag. They roam the countryside, singing, dancing, beating their drums, and blowing their pipes. The Rara perform for money. Their leaders usually dress like jesters and twirl batons. They are accomplished dancers and sometimes challenge dancers from other groups to dancing contests.

During Holy Week, Rara bands carry a picture of Judas from place to place. The picture is hidden on Good Friday, and everybody runs around looking for it. Once the picture is found, it is burned. Burning costumes on the last day of Carnival is also customary, but only the rich can afford to do it. Everybody else reuses his or her costume the next year.

Think about this
Haitians are very poor, so their Carnival costumes require much creativity. A simple straw hat with colorful rags glued to it becomes a flashy headdress. To minimize waste, costumes are carefully packed away to be used again the following year. What other materials might be used to create a low-cost, yet beautiful and elaborate costume?

Rara bands sometimes carry birds, especially chickens, and tin lanterns as they sing and dance in the streets.

VOODOO AND SAUT D'EAU

Africal slaves brought the religion of voodoo to Haiti. Although most Haitians today are Catholic, their ancestral beliefs are still very strong.

These followers of voodoo are in a **trance**, which is an important part of their ritual ceremonies.

What is voodoo?

In Haiti, voodoo is a blend of Catholic rituals and African beliefs. Each voodoo god has an equivalent among the Catholic saints, and voodoo festivals are usually celebrated on the feast days of Catholic saints.

Pilgrimages and feasting

Voodoo festivals are celebrated with much feasting and with pilgrimages to churches dedicated to the saints. Haitians take part in both religious services performed inside the church and voodoo ceremonies carried on outside. One important voodoo pilgrimage is Saut d'Eau. Other voodoo festivals include the feast of Saint Andrew and the feast of Saint Anne.

Loas and life

Haitians believe in powerful spirits known as *loas* [LWA]. Loas supposedly help with everyday problems. In exchange, Haitians "serve" the loas by participating in ceremonies and making food offerings. During a voodoo ceremony, a high priest or priestess will lead the ritual. To be possessed by the loas, Haitians engage in singing, dancing, and drumming. After believers are possessed, their personalities might change, and they might even become aggressive.

During colonial times, when African slaves were not allowed to practice their traditional rituals, they disguised their loas as saints. Hence, voodoo became associated with Catholicism.

Above: Haitians in a voodoo procession march on to worship their god.

Below: Preparing for a voodoo ceremony includes drawing elaborate designs, called *vévés* [VAY-vay], to symbolize the loas.

Above: This service is being held inside a Catholic church during a Saut d'Eau pilgrimage.

Saut d'Eau

Every year, on July 16th, pilgrims gather at Ville-Bonheur to celebrate the appearances of the Virgin Mary in 1843 and 1881. A church now stands on the spot where these appearances occurred. Most pilgrims stop at the church to pray to the Virgin Mary. Then, they go to the Saut d'Eau waterfall. Besides bathing in the pools under the waterfall, they light candles to enlist the help of the ancient spirits believed to live there. As they walk away from the waterfall, they smear their faces with white powder, a sign that they have purified themselves at Saut d'Eau.

Opposite: Bathing in pools under the Saut d'Eau waterfall, voodoo followers tell their sorrows to their gods and hope to wash away bad luck.

Think about this
Zombies are bodies without souls. Haitians are not afraid of zombies because zombies are not evil in themselves. They only act as slaves for their masters. Haitians are terrified most of becoming zombies themselves. To be a zombie means having no control over your own actions, and not having control can be frightening.

FEAST OF SAINT JAMES

Left: A voodoo devotee possessed by Ogou's spirit has covered his body with mud and is in a trance.

Above: A musician at the festival rolls in the mud to honor Ogou.

According to voodoo belief, the Christian Saint James is identified with the voodoo god Ogou, who personifies war. On July 24th, the feast day of Saint James, voodoo groups from all over Haiti make a pilgrimage to the town of Plaine du Nord to honor Ogou. The celebration lasts through the following day. Even Haitians residing in the United States, France, and Guyana do their best to come and participate.

Into the mud

The highlight of the celebration occurs when some of the pilgrims become possessed by the spirit of Ogou and roll around in a pool of mud in one of the streets of Plaine du Nord. These voodoo believers slide or throw themselves into the mud pool and completely cover their bodies with mud.

Other pilgrims standing near the mud pool light candles as an act of worship to Ogou. Sometimes, the voodoo believers also ask Ogou to protect their infants. To do this, the parents of the infant bathe the baby in the mud pool.

A Haitian mother bathes her baby in the mud pool at Plaine du Nord on the feast of Saint James.

Beggars and wishes

As another part of the ceremony, faithful believers of Ogou leave offerings to their god in the pool of mud. Young men carrying large baskets search the pool, digging deep into the mud to find these offerings. They will find coins, rice, and even bits of candles.

A woman who wants Ogou to grant her a wish must **don** her "red-wish," which is an outfit made up of a blue robe, a red scarf, and a red belt with religious medals attached to it. She also carries a staff and a **calabash**. Women wear "red-wish" outfits for a period of time ranging from a few days to three months and ask for wishes, such as a child, a husband, good health, money, or even a visa to the United States.

Above: Women dressed in their "red-wish" stand by the mud pool, while men wade in to dig around for offerings.

The mud pool is the center of the celebration for women, too, on the feast of Saint James.

How it all began

In the late 17th century, settlers in Plaine du Nord chose Saint James as the patron saint of their parish church. When the first African slaves arrived, around the year 1700, the French government would not allow them to practice their African religions and made them attend mass on Sundays. Once, during a mass, the slaves saw a statue of Saint James, which they thought bore a resemblance to their African god, Ogou. The slaves equated Ogou with Saint James, and today's voodoo followers do the same. Although the feast of Saint James is associated with Catholicism, it is voodoo that comes alive in Haiti during this festival.

Think about this

Many voodoo festivals occur on the feast days of Catholic saints, such as the feast of Saint Andrew, which is celebrated on September 30th. Another voodoo festival, which, like the feast of Saint James, is celebrated near Plaine du Nord, is the feast of Saint Anne. This festival, which falls on July 26th, is yet another day and night of eating, drinking, and dancing. There are, however, fewer cases of **possession** by voodoo gods.

These voodoo followers are involved in a lively ceremony to honor their god Ogou.

INDEPENDENCE DAY

January 1st marks both the beginning of the new year and the celebration of freedom for the Haitian people. On January 1, 1804, freedom-fighter Jean-Jacques Dessalines declared independence for the country. Haiti enjoys the status of being the first black republic. Haitians commemorate Independence Day by staging parades and marches.

The importance of independence

Because of the importance of independence, Haiti has two public holidays at the beginning of the year, on January 1st and 2nd. The mood on the morning of January 1st is solemn in memory of the heroes of independence, but the afternoon and the next day are devoted to feasting and rejoicing. Many people continue to celebrate their heroes on January 3rd. These heroes include Toussaint L'Ouverture, Henri Christophe, Jean-Jacques Dessalines, and Alexandre Pétion. (Find out more about these men on pages 22 and 23.)

This young Haitian woman is part of the Independence Day parade.

The Statue of the Maroon

Above: The Citadelle Laferrière in Cap-Haltien was built by one of Haiti's heroes, Henri Christophe.

One of the most poignant moments on January 1st is the laying of wreaths at the foot of the Statue of the Maroon in Port-au-Prince. This morning ceremony is a solemn, formal affair. A maroon is a runaway slave. The Statue of the Maroon represents the freedom that the people of Haiti now enjoy. The wreath-laying ceremony is repeated in all town squares and in front of the National Palace.

The Statue of the Maroon is also a symbol of the strong Haitian spirit in the face of hardship.

A hero to remember

Toussaint L'Ouverture was a slave who gained his freedom in 1777. When a slave revolt broke out in 1791, he joined the rebels and became their leader. Because he had learned to read and write, Toussaint had read many books on how to fight battles. He was clever and managed to outwit his enemies. As a result of this rebellion, Haitian slaves gained their freedom in 1793. Today, Toussaint L'Ouverture is one of Haiti's most celebrated heroes of independence.

During the French Revolution, Toussaint L'Ouverture led the Haitian independence movement. He died in 1803 at about the age of 60.

Leaders of Haiti

Besides Toussaint L'Ouverture, Haiti honors several other important heroes. Toussaint L'Ouverture was eventually captured by the French army, but Haitian army generals, such as Henri Christophe, Jean-Jacques Dessalines, and Alexandre Pétion, continued the fight for independence. When the French tried to restore slavery, the Haitian army, led by these three leaders, fought them off.

In 1804, the land originally known as Saint Domingue was renamed Haiti when Dessalines declared it an independent republic. Later, Christophe held power. He built the Citadelle Laferrière and many palaces.

J.J. DESSALINES
Kaiser auf St. Domingo.

Above: Emperor Jean-Jacques Dessalines ruled Haiti from 1804 to 1806.

This statue is a memorial to Henri Christophe in Port-au-Prince.

Think about this

The people of Haiti look upon those who gave them freedom as heroes. All Haitian children know and respect the memory of Toussaint L'Ouverture, Henri Christophe, Jean-Jacques Dessalines, and Alexandre Pétion. Do you have a favorite historical hero who changed the lives of the people in your country?

THE DAY OF THE DEAD

In the Christian calendar, November 2nd, All Souls' Day, is devoted to remembering and honoring the dead. The Day of the Dead is one of the most important holidays in Haiti. Because of their voodoo tradition, the people of Haiti feel very close to the dead and revere them. On November 2nd, Haitians visit the graves of their dead relatives and friends, carrying flowers and candles. They clean the tombstones, decorate the graves with flowers, light candles, and say prayers. Some families set up a small shrine at home, complete with candles and a picture of the dead relative.

These Haitians are praying for their loved ones who have passed away.

The family of the deceased will decorate this grave with flowers.

Voodoo followers celebrate the Day of the Dead.

Feeding the dead

Another custom Haitian families observe on November 2nd is offering food to their dead relatives, or ***manger aux morts*** [mahn-djay oh MORE], meaning "food for the dead." Before a family sits down to dinner, they put a plate of food for the dead relative on the ground or set it on the table at the place where the dead person used to sit. Then they light a candle and say prayers for the dead person. In the villages, however, people prefer to eat their dinners first, then leave the leftovers for the dead.

Lords of death

The voodoo spirits, or loas, who possess believers on the Day of the Dead are called the ***Gede*** [gay-DAY]. They wander through streets and cemeteries dressed to look like corpses or undertakers.

THINGS FOR YOU TO DO

Haitians are very artistic people. Examples of Haitian art can be seen throughout the country on buses, churches, houses, government buildings, and even lampposts—all brightly decorated with scenes and patterns in vivid colors. Haitian art is unique and combines the art of African ancestors with French influence.

Taptaps

Haiti's colorful public buses, called *taptaps* [TAP-taps], are old trucks or vans converted into mobile works of art. They are covered with brightly colored paintings of flowers, animals, geometric shapes, and spaceships and are decorated with diamonds and stars. Religious phrases are often written on the sides of the taptaps, illuminated by colored lights.

Haiti's taptaps are not only one of the most colorful and elaborate forms of public transportation in Latin America and the Caribbean; they are also brilliant examples of the artistic talent of the Haitian people. As the most popular form of public transportation in Haiti, they are often filled with children, animals, and adults carrying baskets of vegetables and fruit.

Create a Haitian work of art

Haitian artistic style varies widely. There are over 800 recognized painters in Haiti, each with a style of his or her own. One of the best known Haitian painters is DeWitt Peters, who invented a style of painting that uses striking colors to illustrate the everyday life of the Haitian people. Many modern Haitian painters specialize in geometric shapes using vivid colors, as in the painting pictured above.

You can make a painting like the one above. All you need is a large piece of art paper, a pencil, a ruler, paintbrushes, and brightly colored paints, such as red, yellow, blue, orange, and green. Copy this design or create a design of your own. Just remember to paint your design in the brightest colors!

Things to look for in your library

Caribbean Destinations: Haiti. (http://www.caribbeansupersite.com/haiti/).
Crisis in Haiti (Headliners). Meish Goldish (Millbrook Press, 1995).
Haiti: Haiti Sings. (compact disc).
Haiti: Waters of Sorrow. (Turner Home Entertainment, 1991).
The Magic Orange Tree and Other Haitian Folktales. Diane Wolkstein (Schocken Books, 1997).
Running the Road to ABC. Denize Lauture (Simon & Schuster, 1996).
Tap-Tap. Karen L. Williams (Clarion Books, 1994).
Toussaint L'Ouverture: The Fight for Haiti's Freedom. Walter D. Myers (Simon & Schuster, 1996).

MAKE A CARNIVAL HEADDRESS

Haitians make clever Carnival outfits. Part of each outfit is the headdress. To make your own Carnival headdress, all you need is an old straw hat, some colored paper, glue, and a ribbon. Do you want to try?

5

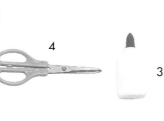
4

3

2

1

You will need:
1. A straw hat with a 4-inch (10-cm) brim
2. Large sheets of crepe paper in a variety of bright colors
3. Glue
4. Scissors
5. A piece of colorful cloth

1 Cut all of the crepe paper into long strips.

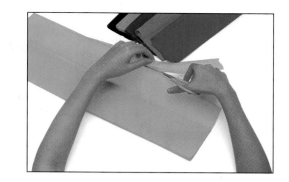

2 On each strip of crepe paper, make a fold every 2 inches (5 cm) along the entire strip. Fold all of the strips this way.

3 Use glue to attach the edge of each strip to the brim of the hat. After you have glued all the strips to the hat, open out the folds of the strips.

4 To make the hat even brighter and more decorative, tie a piece of colorful cloth around it. Now, you have your very own Carnival headdress. Why not teach your friends how to make one, too!

MAKE BLANCMANGE

Haitians have a sweet tooth, so they love *blancmange* [blahn-MAHNGE]. Richly flavored with coconut, this light dessert is a favorite of both adults and children. Be careful when boiling the mixture. Always have an adult help you with the steps in this recipe!

You will need:

1. 1½ cups (360 ml) coconut cream
2. 1½ cups (360 ml) evaporated milk
3. 1½ cups (360 ml) sweetened condensed milk
4. 1 tablespoon unflavored gelatin
5. ½ cup (114 g) flaked coconut
6. 1 tablespoon sugar
7. Bowl
8. Saucepan
9. Wooden spoon
10. Measuring cup
11. Measuring spoons
12. Oven mitt or potholder
13. Non-stick baking sheet

1 Pour 1 cup (240 milliliters) of water into the saucepan. Heat the water and dissolve the gelatin in it. Add the coconut cream, evaporated milk, and condensed milk. Bring the mixture to a boil over moderate heat, stirring constantly.

2 Remove the saucepan from the heat and immediately pour the mixture into a bowl. Let it cool at room temperature, then refrigerate it for at least four hours.

3 Preheat the oven to broil. Cover the bottom of a non-stick baking sheet with coconut flakes and sprinkle sugar over them. Place the baking sheet under the broiler for 5 to 10 minutes until the coconut flakes are golden brown. Remove the baking sheet from the oven and let the coconut cool.

4 Just before serving, top the blancmange with the toasted coconut.

GLOSSARY

bandes-à-pieds, 9	Groups of musicians that walk through the streets singing and dancing during Carnival.
calabash, 18	A type of gourd.
don, 18	To put on (as clothing).
Gede, 25	Voodoo spirits that possess people on November 2nd, All Souls' Day, or the Day of the Dead.
lamayote, 10	A small box containing a "pet" that children show off during Carnival to get a few coins.
manger aux morts, 25	The custom of offering food to dead relatives on All Souls' Day, or the Day of the Dead.
possession, 19	The state in which a person's mind and body is controlled by an outside force or spirit.
trance, 12	A dazed state of awareness accompanied by an inability to move or act.
voodoo, 3	A religion that combines elements of the Roman Catholic faith with African beliefs.

INDEX

Picture credits
A. N. A. Press Agency: 16 (both), 17, 18 (both); Camera Press Ltd.: 5; DDB Stock Photo: 7 (bottom), 9 (top), 10 (both), 24 (top), 27; HBL Network Photo Agency: 11, 19; Dave G. Houser: 26; Hutchison Library: 8, 9 (bottom), 13 (top), 21 (top), 24 (bottom), 28; Bjorn Klingwall: 25; Life File: 1; North Wind Picture Archives: 22 (bottom), 23 (top); David Simson: 2, 3 (bottom), 4, 6; Still Pictures: 12, 13 (bottom); Times Editions: 3 (top), 14, 15, 20; Topham Picture Point: 7 (top), 21 (bottom), 22 (top), 23 (bottom)

Digital scanning by
Superskill Graphics Pte Ltd.